∞

The Good Galilean

Also by Alban Goodier
from Sophia Institute Press®:

Saints for Sinners

Archbishop Alban Goodier

The Good Galilean

Lessons in Living from the Son of Man Himself

SOPHIA INSTITUTE PRESS®
Manchester, New Hampshire

The Good Galilean was originally published in 1928 by The Macmillan Company, New York, under the title *Jesus Christ, the Model of Manhood.* This slightly abridged 2009 edition by Sophia Institute Press® includes minor editorial revisions and does not include the introduction in the original edition.

Cover design by Theodore Schluenderfritz

On the cover: *Christ in the House of Martha and Mary,*
by Jan Vermeer, National Gallery of Scotland,
Edinburgh, Scotland / The Bridgeman Art Library

Sophia Institute Press®
Box 5284, Manchester, NH 03108
1-800-888-9344
www.SophiaInstitute.com

Nihil obstat: Arthur J. Scanlan, S.T.D., *Censor Librorum*
Imprimatur: Patrick Cardinal Hayes, Archbishop, New York
New York, December 22, 1927

Library of Congress Cataloging-in-Publication Data

Goodier, Alban, 1869-1939.
    The good Galilean : lessons in living from the Son of Man himself / by Alban Goodier.
        p. cm.
    Rev. ed. of: Jesus Christ, the model of manhood.
    ISBN 978-1-928832-60-7 (pbk. : alk. paper) 1. Jesus Christ — Example. 2. Christian life — Catholic authors. I. Goodier, Alban, 1869-1939. Jesus Christ, the model of manhood. II. Title.
    BT304.2.G66 2009
    232.9'04 — dc22

                                                          2009035631

Contents

∞

∞

The Good Galilean

Editor's note: The biblical quotations in the following pages are taken from the Douay-Rheims edition of the Old and New Testaments. Where applicable, quotations have been cross-referenced with the differing names and enumeration in the Revised Standard Version, using the following symbol: (RSV =).

Introduction

∞

The Perfect Man

Many philosophers in the past, many novelists and poets in more recent times, have attempted to describe for us the perfect man. From the very nature of the case, their descriptions have differed one from another; while, perhaps, all have been good so far as they have gone, none have been able to include in their description the whole idea of man's perfection. For man is limited and finite; he cannot conceive in his mind an ideal that contains in itself the whole scope of perfection, not even if his vision confines itself to the plane of nature alone.

And even if he could, when he comes to describe it, he can do so only in the limited terms of his own imagination and language. He will speak from his own experience of himself, especially his own shortcomings, from his knowledge of and insight into other men, possibly from the ideal picture that his imagination has conjured up after the

The Good Galilean

sordidness of real life has been eliminated. But in every case it will be his own vision and perspective, his own point of view, which will be expressed; true, noble, complete, perfect in its degree, but nevertheless with the confining limitations and lacunae that human nature cannot escape. In fact or in fiction, in history or in drama, the altogether perfect man does not exist; if he did, if he were in all things and always perfect, he would be something more than human.

So we say, speaking of ourselves and of one another, of all men as we know them, of all men as they have been described by others; the knowledge of this truth leads us to judge not, that we may not be judged, to forgive as we would be forgiven, to see not the mote in our brother's eye, being only too conscious of the beam within in our own. Human nature, because it is human nature, is faulty.

And yet we are compelled to make one exception. There has lived in this world one man in whom, if he is taken wholly, no fault whatsoever has been found, who has shown himself in all things perfect, whose accurate picture, moreover, has been handed down for us all to study; the impossible has been done before our eyes. The more closely the portrait is examined, and the more in detail the character is revealed, so much the more is this amazing fact found to be true; and not only by followers who love his name, and might therefore be predisposed to see in him "the most beautiful of the sons of men,"[1] but by unbelievers also, who would look on him with cold eyes, unenthusiastic in his cause, what they would call unprejudiced and scientific, and yet would be honest and sincere. They have scrutinized Jesus, the Carpenter of Nazareth, and have found him to be "the Lamb of God," "the King of Israel."[2] They have listened to and sifted his words, and have acknowledged that "never did man speak as this man spoke."[3] They have weighed all his deeds and have declared that "he hath done all things well."[4] They have compared him with others and have concluded, "We have never seen the like."[5] They have looked for a charge against him and have owned with Pilate, "I find no fault in this just man."[6] They have pierced his heart, and what they have found there has made them confess: "Indeed this was the Son of God."[7]

[1] Cf. Ps. 44:3 (RSV = 45:2).
[2] John 1:29, 49.
[3] Cf. John 7:46.
[4] Mark 7:37.
[5] Mark 2:12.
[6] Cf. Luke 23:4.
[7] Matt. 27:54.

The Good Galilean

This conclusion, however vague in its final expression, we may well be justified in claiming as the glorious outcome of the long-drawn battle that a century and more has seen waged around the name of Jesus Christ. Whatever adverse and less enlightened criticism might have attempted in the past, whatever specious science might attempt today, sober scholarship the world over comes more and more to acknowledge this at least: not only the full fact of Jesus Christ as the Scriptures give him to us, not only that he stands out pre-eminently as the greatest man this world has ever seen, but also the further fact that he is so great, so complete, so universally perfect as to be unique, in some sublime sense more than ordinary man either is, or could be, or could ever of himself fashion in his mind.

Students have naturally looked for limitations, and have found none; some have assumed shortcomings, and others have proved their assumptions to be contrary to the facts. They have searched for the shadows corresponding to his established virtues, and have found them not to be there; powers and gifts that in other men do not co-exist are discovered united in him. He is undefinable; limited though he may be because of his humanity, still we cannot fix the limits; if we try to lay hands on him, if we say that because he is this therefore he is not that, he slips through our fingers and escapes us. No one quality can be ascribed to him as characteristic to the exclusion of another; he possesses them all. The ideal that man of himself cannot so much as imagine has been found in him in real life. We live in an age of discoveries, but no discovery of our time has been more momentous, more epoch-making, than this.

∞

We must see Jesus as both God and man

It is not that we have discovered anything we have not known before; fortunately for the world, the knowledge of Jesus Christ never has been and never can be lost. Rather, it is the angle of vision that may be considered comparatively new. From the days of St. Paul, it has been well understood that Jesus Christ, the true Son of God, since he chose to become man, could not but be perfect man. Since he came for man, for man's redemption and to be man's model, he could not but be man's perfect model. Given the Godhead and the truth of the Scriptures, there was only one light in which those Scriptures could be read by the Fathers and the early Church, and that was "the Light which was the life of men, the true Light, which enlighteneth every man that cometh into this world."[8]

[8] Cf. John 1:9.

The Good Galilean

But in our own time, the tendency has been to begin at the opposite extreme; to argue not from the Godhead to the manhood, but from the manhood to wherever the argument might lead. It was a course inevitable for those to whom God had come to have little or no meaning, who were therefore compelled to investigate the facts of history as historical facts alone, incapable of being anything more. Since the Sonship of God to them meant nothing, the truth had to be read and interpreted by them in the absence of that guiding light; and although, even in that darkness, the picture obtained of Jesus Christ has been of surpassing human beauty, yet has it fallen far short of the whole.

By way of contrast and example, compare the *Life of Jesus Christ* by Ludolph of Saxony, written in the fifteenth century, and the life by Renan in the nineteenth; the life by Ludolph still lives, while that by Renan, with all its charm, has been long repudiated, by none more than by his own disciples.

The same tendency has been followed, and seems now to be increasingly followed, by another school. To this school God is indeed a great reality, but it has made so much of the *kenosis*, the "emptying out" of the God-made-man, as virtually to assume that Jesus, if he is rightly to be understood, must be studied as being man only, prescinding entirely, or almost entirely, from his divinity. To this school would seem to belong an ever-growing number of English Protestant writers today. To it the Jesus of history must be considered apart from the Jesus of faith; where history records a fact, that fact must be understood as man by his experience understands it and no more. In this restricted light, much of necessity has been distorted. Jesus Christ, considered as man and man only, whatever might lie hidden in the background, forced into the mold of other men, has rendered disconcerting conclusions. Many words and actions and events in the Gospels have been surrendered; their riddle can be read only when his own full light has been turned upon them. And yet, even to this school, in spite of its assertion of his ignorance, his groping to the discovery of himself, and other limitations put upon him, he stands out as a perfect being, unique, more than man.

But in this simple exposition of the Catholic mind, or rather, let us say of one single aspect of the Catholic mind, in regard to Jesus Christ, there is neither room nor need for controversy. Except perchance by way of confirmation, we need not dwell upon the opinions of others. We stand on sure ground, we walk along paths that have long been well trodden, and from whatever goal men of good-will set out, they arrive in the end at the same center. Jesus

The Good Galilean

Christ, being God, is also as man the model of perfect manhood. Jesus Christ, being man, is found to be more than man, is found to be what he declared himself to be, the true Son of God made truly man, yet remaining one with the Father. In this way, the revelation grew upon those who first learned to read the Carpenter of Nazareth; when they had read him, the overwhelming truth took hold of them, and in the light of the Godhead, the manhood became more manifestly clear. Thus does the one truth reflect upon and clarify the other; the Light that is the life of men is the Word made flesh; the Word made flesh is the Light of the world, whose "glory we have seen, the glory as it were of the only-begotten of the Father, full of grace and truth."[9]

[9] John 1:14.

Chapter 1

∞

What the Gospels Tell Us About Jesus

When we read the four Gospels with attention, one thing at least must strike us of their respective authors: the conviction deep down in them all that every word they wrote was true. There is no attempt to emphasize what they have to say, as will one who narrates the naturally incredible, or who is eager to convince either himself or his audience. Miracles are told with the same simplicity as other events; in dealing with the central figure, they pass from the sublime to the commonplace with disconcerting ease. But in regard to that central figure, this has a wonderful effect: it is alive; it walks out of its surroundings and stands apart; it detaches itself, it would seem, from its own generation and walks through all ages, belongs to all time.

Before any attempt is made to draw out the features of this portrait, it will be well, for the sake of a background, to look at the life of Jesus as a whole. Of the earliest phase

The Good Galilean

little need be said: that phase of miraculous promise, of "good tidings of great joy"[10] and yet of humble infancy, of that combination of joy and sorrow, adoration and subject helplessness, submission to the Law and yet supremacy, command and obedience, which at once prepares us for the paradoxes, the seemingly impossible contrasts, which mark his whole career. The period closes with his first recorded words: "Did you not know that I must be about my Father's business?"[11] They are the motto of his life.

Until he was thirty years of age, all we are told is that "he was subject to them"; that "he grew and waxed strong, full of wisdom, and the grace of God was in him"; and that he "advanced in wisdom, and age, and grace before God and men."[12] At the age of thirty, he came down to the Jordan, a sinner it would have seemed among sinners, to be baptized by John. From the Jordan he again passes out of sight into the desert; not only will he be accounted a sinner among sinners, but, like every sinner, he will be tempted even as they.

So completely is this willingness to be unknown and unnoticed a part of his nature, that not until he is revealed

---

[10] Luke 2:10.

[11] Luke 2:49.

[12] Luke 2:40, 51, 52.

by John, and not until some followers of John, of their own accord, come to him, does he make the least effort to be found. But as soon as they come, then follows a quick response. They are welcomed as dear companions. By mere contact with him they are stirred with an enthusiasm they had never known before. Instantly they go away and bring others to him. The fascination captures them all, and they long to be with him always. And Jesus rewards them; he takes them with him into Galilee; before their eyes he turns water into wine. Back he comes with them to Jerusalem, and again before their eyes he drives out the buyers and sellers from the Temple. They learn from the beginning what he can do, what power over things and men is behind this Carpenter of Nazareth. They have begun in love; they are at once led on to faith and trust.

Nevertheless, so long as John the Baptist is in the field, Jesus is content to bide his time and wait; not until the Precursor is taken and clapped into prison does he show himself before the world. But when that deed is done, he begins to move. With a daring that defies all opposition, of Pharisees and doctors of the Law, of Herod and all his myrmidons, of ignorant Galileans and all their prejudices, of dwellers in Jerusalem and all their bigotry, he comes out boldly and proclaims that the Kingdom is at hand, and that he, Jesus, is the messenger sent to found it. From this moment he moves quickly and surely. There is no hesitation in his method, no drawing back because of opposition. His own men of Nazareth reject him, and at once he calls others to his aid; the people of Capernaum accept him, and he pours out upon them all he has to give in a very torrent. Pharisees set themselves to catch him in word or deed, and before their eyes he proves his power, not only of healing, but of forgiving sins.

This first outburst of authority carries all before him; men look on and ask themselves, "What thing is this? What is this new doctrine? What word is this? For with authority and power he commandeth even the unclean spirits, and they obey him and go out."[13] "And all the multitudes were astonished and filled with fear and wondered and glorified God that gave such power to men."[14]

Endurance of friends, and equal endurance of enemies; forbearance, silent and ignoring, with those who knew no better; encouragement, gentle, cheerful, happy, fascinating, to those from whom he hoped for and expected more; equally considerate to rich and poor, learned and unlearned, sophisticated citizens of Judea and narrow

[13] Mark 1:27; Luke 4:36.

[14] Matt. 9:8; Mark 2:12; Luke 5:26.

countryfolk of Galilee, Pharisees and publicans, rulers in the city and lepers on the road, disciples and strangers, believers and harsh critics; intimate with all but depending on none, appealing to them to believe in him, but not despondent if he failed; giving all he had to give if they would but receive it, inviting all, refusing none, striking friends and rivals dumb by his lavish and unconditional generosity; and when abused for the gifts he gave, never closing up his hand, sparing himself in nothing, although he knew that the seed he sowed fell on stony or thorn-choked soil; and underneath, like a thundering, awful, underground torrent, a life apart and independent of prayer and spiritual understanding that could not be ruffled by the gales and storms upon the surface: such is an impression of Jesus in the first and most active, yet perhaps the least self-revealing, period of his public life.

∞

The confession of Peter

So he prepared the ground. Then up on the hill behind Capernaum, after a whole night spent in prayer, he called to himself his Twelve Apostles, choosing "whom he would himself,"[15] and no man should interfere or deny him. It

[15] Mark 3:13; Luke 6:12 ff.

15

was an act of high command. It was followed by that momentous sermon, the charter of the new Kingdom, the challenge thrown in his own name to all the world.[16] This again was confirmed by deeds of singular mercy: by praise and reward of a pagan's faith, by singular pity for a widowed mother's tears, by the befriending of a "woman in the city, a sinner" whom no self-respecting man would touch, by permitting that women should come with him, to help him in his need.[17]

And yet it was not all victory. Indeed, at every turn he met with disappointment. Already from the first, by the Jordan in Judaea, suspicion and jealousy had hunted him out; now in Galilee he was not to be left alone.

His rivals could not do what he did; therefore, must he be proved a deceiver. He went about doing good; therefore, must he be stopped: "And they were filled with madness; and they talked one with another, what they might do to Jesus."[18] He spoke "as one having authority"; therefore, he was a blasphemer: "'Who is this who speaketh blasphemies?'"[19] The miracles could not be denied;

[16] Matt. 5-7.

[17] Matt. 8:5-18; Luke 7:1, 11-17, 36-50; 8:1-3.

[18] Luke 6:11.

[19] Luke 5:21.

therefore, in them must be found ground for accusation. He did them on the Sabbath day, and thereby broke the Sabbath;[20] he did them by no human power, and thereby proved that he was himself possessed: "This man hath Beelzebub, and casteth out devils by the prince of devils."[21]

And to some extent, as must always be the case, the people were influenced by these insinuations of their leaders. They, too, began to wonder and to doubt. From this time we see him turning more and more away from them, as they turned more away from him. He still has deep compassion for them, for they are lying "like sheep that have no shepherd";[22] he still lets them crowd about him and jostle him in the streets.[23] But he knows that not on them can the Kingdom be founded. He must attend more and more to the Twelve. To them apart, from henceforth, he gives special instructions;[24] for them alone he works special miracles, stirring them to ever more faith,[25]

---

[20] Matt. 12:9-14; Mark 3:1-6; Luke 6:1-11.

[21] Matt. 12:24; Mark 3:22.

[22] Matt. 9:35-38; Mark 6:6.

[23] Mark 5:31; Luke 8:45.

[24] Matt. 13:11; Mark 4:11; Luke 13:10.

[25] Matt. 8:23-27; Mark 4:35-41; Luke 8:22-25.

The Good Galilean

filling them at once with awe and confidence,[26] before them allowing his simple childlike affection to appear in the midst of his weary disappointment,[27] endowing them with his own powers and sending them forth so that they may learn in practice the work to which they have been called.[28]

They went out over Galilee while he remained at home. They preached; they worked wonders in his name; they came back happy men. They came to him like children to one who understood them, and told him all that they had done; they rejoiced with him and he rejoiced with them.[29] In spite of the gathering of the gloom about him, in spite of the threats and warnings that of late had been coming from his lips, he had not lost, he never lost, that inward peace and fascination and familiarity by which those about him were made glad.

Never throughout his life does Jesus lose that trait. If he is roused to anger, the next instant proves that he is always controlled; if he is stung to the quick, however he may show that he feels it, there is never any change in his

[26] Matt. 8:28-34; Mark 5:1-20; Luke 8:26-39.

[27] Matt. 9:23-26; Mark 5:35-43; Luke 8:49-56.

[28] Matt. 10:5-15; Mark 6:7-13; Luke 9:1-6.

[29] Mark 6:30; Luke 9:10.

heart. Once only, at the end, in the Garden of Gethsemane, does the cloud seem to enclose him altogether; but even then his will is bent to the will of his Father, and he can face his death with calm.

The first period, of wonders and success, had led up to the choosing of the Twelve and the Sermon on the Mount; the second, of reaction, had been marked by the instruction of the Twelve apart from all the rest. He would close it with a new high-water mark. He drew his best apart into the desert; there he fed them, five thousand men, besides women and children; he stirred their zeal until they called him "the prophet," and would hail him as their king.[30] In the plain of Genesareth, by a yet more lavish outpouring of miracles, he deepened the impression.

Then, when they at last professed their allegiance as they had never professed it before, he gave them the one test of all; he offered them his flesh to eat, and his blood to drink. And at this last moment, they failed him; in spite of all they had received, in spite of all they had promised, they failed him. "Many of his disciples, hearing it, said, This saying is hard, and who shall hear it?" And "after this, many of his disciples went back, and walked with him no more."[31]

[30] John 6:14-15.
[31] John 6:61, 67 (RSV = John 6:60, 66).

The Good Galilean

Jesus left Capernaum with a saddened heart; we do not hear that he ever set foot in it again. He had made the one great offer for which all these months he had been preparing, and it had been rejected; the one offer which, had they but shut their eyes to their own questionings and accepted the truth of him that was all true, would have revealed to those men the wealth of power and love and generosity that was within their grasp, and which was more than belonged to any mortal man to give. He left the place; he left Galilee; he went out of the land of the Jews into pagan Tyre and Sidon.

For months he wandered abroad, keeping the Twelve continually with him, giving to them in this alien land an utterly new outlook on life. Since the mission on which he had sent them through Galilee, there had been a long respite: miracles were few, and they were less spontaneous than before; preaching very little, and that with a continued note of warning; avoidance but not fear of his enemies, for when he met them, he defied them to their faces; prayer and solitude in abundance; all the time a deepening upon them of personal influence, in familiarity along with dignity, leaving through these hot summer months the seed he had sown to grow within their hearts. More and more he had confined himself to them; at length, the time came when their faith, too, must be finally tested.

"And it came to pass in the way, as he was alone praying, his disciples also were with him, and he asked them, 'Who do the people say that I am? Who do men say that the Son of man is?' "

They gave him an answer that now concerned him little. Then he asked, " 'But who do you say that I am?' Simon Peter answered and said, 'Thou art Christ, the Son of the living God.' "[32] It was enough; at last, by a single man on earth, with the light of the Father from heaven, he had been discovered and owned for what he was. There and then, upon that man, the Church of God was founded; henceforth, it mattered little what Pharisees or doctors might say or do. His work was now assured; now he could march on boldly to his death.

∞

To Palm Sunday

With the confession of Peter, Jesus' manner seemed completely to change. At once he cut short his wanderings into foreign lands. He returned to Galilee; on Mount Tabor, to reward them for their faith, and to prepare them for what was yet to come, he showed to three of them a shadow of his Godhead. For a month or thereabouts, he

[32] Matt. 16:13-16; Mark 8:27-29; Luke 9:18-20.

The Good Galilean

still hung about the upper province. But he seemed no longer to care to preach. He no longer busied himself with miracles; instead, he took means to hide himself away, content only with deepening the faith of his Twelve, strengthening them for the great ordeal that would soon be upon them.

Nevertheless, how little, after all, did these poor men from Galilee understand! In many places we are reminded of their ignorance, even at this late hour;[33] patience and forbearance he had to show them to the end, perhaps more at the end than in the early days of hope and promise. And not only to his own; he had to show it also to his enemies. One might say that the rest of his life is but a continued manifestation of unwearied patience and long-suffering to all who came within its range.

On the Feast of Tabernacles, he marched again into Jerusalem. Let his enemies do what they would, he stayed there all the time, moving in and out of the Temple as he pleased. He came again for the Feast of Dedication; in the intervals, he remained for the most part in the neighborhood, in Judea or Perea, for any of his foes to meet him who chose. The atmosphere is heavy with storm; his death is continually on the lips of men; more than one

[33] Mark 9:32 ff.

attempt is made to take him; we need to bear all this in mind if we would understand aright the depth, warmth, and all-enduring patience of his last appeals.

- "'If any man thirst, let him come to me and drink."[34]

- "I am the light of the world. He that followeth me walketh not in darkness, but shall have the light of life."[35]

- "I am the good shepherd. The good shepherd giveth his life for his sheep."[36]

- "I am the good shepherd, and I know mine, and mine know me."[37]

- "Come to me all you that labor and are burdened, and I will refresh you. Take my yoke upon you, and learn of me, because I am meek and humble of heart; and you shall find rest for your souls. For my yoke is sweet, and my burden light."[38]

[34] John 7:37.
[35] John 8:12.
[36] John 10:11.
[37] John 10:14.
[38] Matt. 11:28-30.

The Good Galilean

With language such as this, Jesus fought his great campaign against his bitterest enemies in Jerusalem, only a few months before he died. It was the forgiveness of "seventy times seven times"[39] put into practice. Such enduring forbearance could never have been invented; the whole story teems with emotion, the man who speaks has his heart full. Incredible bearing of abuse and insult and trickery, understanding sympathy with friends and foes, quick response to any least sign of recognition, fascinating imagery linking his words with all around him, firm, consistent assertion of the truth that seemed to compel belief, exact interpretation of the past, clear and unflinching vision of the future, seeing at once both death and victory, beneath it all peace and assurance and strength in the knowledge and love and intimate union with the Father: all this was evident to all, and portrayed a soul so perfect as to be more than human. His enemies knew even better than his friends what it implied.

With this last cry, one might almost say, the portrait of Jesus for our present purpose is completed. It is strong as a tower yet delicate as a feather; yielding as a blade of grass to every breath of wind, yet firm as a rock before the heaviest wash of water. For the rest, the Evangelists, chiefly St.

[39] Matt. 18:22.

Luke, are content merely to touch in the lights and shadows, all in keeping with this last impression.

For instance, soon after this, down the highroad from the city, a lawyer asks Jesus what is the great commandment of the Law, and he is made to answer his own question — that it is the love of God and the love of one's neighbor. He asks who is his neighbor, and he is given that perfect story, of the Good Samaritan.[40] At this time, we find him accepting hospitality from two simple women of Bethany;[41] at this time, he is found alone in prayer, and by his example makes others long to pray like him;[42] at this time, he sees a poor, aged woman bent double, and, unasked, puts his gentle hand upon her and makes her stand up straight.[43] While the enmity about him grows ever more bitter, while he is compelled to become ever more emphatic in his retort, nevertheless precisely at this time, and it would seem precisely in proportion, does his tenderness of heart reveal itself, in the parables of the Lost Sheep and of the Prodigal Son,[44] in his weeping over the

[40] Luke 10:25-37.
[41] Luke 10:38-42.
[42] Luke 11:1-13.
[43] Luke 13:10-17.
[44] Luke 15:1-7, 11-32.

tomb of his friend Lazarus, and his raising him to life,[45] in his healing of the ten lepers, and his expression of regret that only one came back to thank him,[46] in the parable of the Pharisee and the Publican,[47] in the welcome he gave to the little children and their mothers,[48] in the love he showed to the young man who fain would follow him: "Jesus looked on him and loved him,"[49] in the hearty, even merry greeting to the publican Zachaeus,[50] and, last of all, in the defense he made of the woman who poured out upon him of her best.[51]

∞

To the Passion

That last scene ended all; the rest was but the conclusion of the tragedy. In the triumphant procession of palms, Jesus told the world that he was its Master.[52] On the next

[45] John 11:1-46.

[46] Luke 17:12-19.

[47] Luke 18:9-14.

[48] Matt. 19:13-15; Mark 10:13-16; Luke 18:15-17.

[49] Matt. 19:16; Mark 10:17; Luke 18:18.

[50] Luke 19:1-10.

[51] Matt. 26:6-13; Mark 14:3-9; John 12:1-11.

[52] Matt. 21:1-11; Mark 11:1-11; Luke 19:29-44; John 12:12-19.

day, when again he cleansed the Temple, he told the priests and the doctors of the Law that he was their Master, too.[53] For two days more, he came into their midst and let them gather around him. He permitted them to harry him with bickerings and questions, as they had never harried him before. With a power at once noble and crushing, he silenced them, every one, so that from that time forward, they dared ask him no more questions.[54]

Then, with an eloquence that is unsurpassed, he pronounced upon them their doom.[55] With that he passed out of the Temple, never to enter it again. On the hillside of Olivet, he warned his own of the evil days that would be.[56] He retired to Bethany, and there he hid himself away, preparing for the last great surrender.

In what follows, although, through it all, the character of Jesus is seen as it is seen nowhere else, we must be content to move quickly. It was paschal time, the last of his life, and a place must be found in which he might celebrate it; although on other nights he had yielded to his enemies and fled the city, on this night, being the King he

[53] Matt. 21:12-17; Mark 11:15-19; Luke 19:45-48.
[54] Matt. 22:46.
[55] Matt. 23:1-39.
[56] Matt. 24:25; Mark 13; Luke 21:5-36.

was, the Son of David proclaimed on the Sunday preceding, he would choose for this ever-memorable ceremony a noble mansion in the noblest quarter of the town, under the very walls of Annas and Caiphas, and not a soul would deny him.[57] When the hour arrived, he would go up with his own, and to them alone he would reveal the secret of his heart; this last bequest he would leave to them before he died, the key to all that had gone before, and to all that was to come after.

"Before the festival day of the pasch, Jesus, knowing that his hour was come, and that he should pass out of this world to the Father, having loved his own that were in the world, he loved them unto the end."[58]

He sat down with them at table; restlessly he rose and washed their feet; his heart fluttered at the remembrance that in spite of all he was to them, and of all they were to him, one among them would betray him, another would deny him, and all would desert him in his hour of need. Still he would not stay his hand. For them he had never before stayed it; he would not do it then. Instead, even to them, even at this hour of utter disappointment, he would surpass himself in generosity. He gave them his flesh to

[57] Matt. 26:17-19; Mark 14:12-16; Luke 22:7-13.
[58] John 13:1.

eat; he gave them his blood to drink. He gave himself to them for all time, that they might eat him and drink him when they chose, and, when they chose, give him to be food and drink to others. He gave as only God could give, and only the God of utter love.[59]

Love and service, mastership and lowly submission: we have seen them manifested all through his life, but never more conspicuously than now. Sensitive agony because of desertion, overwhelming gratitude because of the least recognition, sadness unto death because of failure, encouragement because of the certainty of victory beyond all these lights and shadows play upon his soul during all that supper night; but always in the end love conquers, and always to these men, no matter what they might then be, no matter what they might soon do, there is nothing but hope and encouragement, and love and sympathy poured out. They will be separated from him, but let them not mind: he will not leave them orphans; he will come back to them. They will be scandalized in him, but let them not mind: he has prayed for them, for Simon in particular, and all will yet be well. They will be hated by the world, but let them not mind: the world has hated him before them. They will be persecuted by men; to put them to death will

[59] Matt. 26:26-29; Mark 14:22-25; Luke 22:19-20.

be deemed a duty, but let them not mind: he himself has overcome the world; the prince of this world is already conquered.

Even that is not enough. Such consolation is only negative, and Jesus can never stop there. They are his own, he loves them to the end, and they must partake of his reward. "With a strong cry and tears"[60] he makes to his Father a further claim, and it is based on an argument that no man but he, the Son of God made man, could make.

"I have glorified thee on the earth: I have finished the work thou gavest me to do."[61]

He had lived a perfect life; the manhood had corresponded with the Godhead; while other men had to learn "Forgive us our trespasses," he could with truth say this only of himself and, because of it, could ask of his Father what he would. And what did he ask? For himself, nothing; for them, everything: that these, his own, should be preserved from evil; that they should be made one among themselves; that they should be forever one with him; "that the love wherewith thou hast loved me may be in them, and I in them."[62]

[60] Heb. 5:7.
[61] John 17:4.
[62] John 17:26.

What the Gospels Tell Us About Jesus

That was the final goal. We take that last expression of his soul and look back, and in the light of it all, the life of Jesus is aglow with a new significance. This is his Kingdom, as he himself esteems it; for this he has labored all the time; to satisfy his own outpouring love for men, to win their love to himself, to stir within them a love for one another such as mankind has never known before.

Chapter 2

∞

Jesus Is Perfect in Himself

"It behooved him in all things to be made like unto his brethren, that he might become a merciful and faithful high priest before God, that he might be a propitiation for the sins of the people. For in that wherein he himself hath suffered and been tempted he is able to succor them also that are tempted."[63]

"For we have not a high priest who cannot have compassion on our infirmities, but one tempted in all things like as we are, without sin . . . Who in the days of his flesh, with a strong cry and tears, offering up prayers and supplications to him that was able to save him from death, was heard for his reverence. And whereas indeed he was the Son of God, he learned obedience by the things which he suffered."[64]

[63] Heb. 2:17-18.
[64] Heb. 4:15; 5:7-8.

The Good Galilean

"'It was fitting that we should have a high priest, holy, innocent, undefiled, separated from sinners, and made higher than the heavens.'"[65]

In these and many other passages of the later New Testament, we are shown how the real humanity of Jesus Christ, with all its limitations and weaknesses, remained impressed, after he was gone, upon the minds of his first disciples. When the whole picture had been completed, then, and then only, they saw the significance of all its parts. Then at last they realized the meaning of that lowliness and meekness which in his lifetime, especially at the latter end, had tended to be to them a scandal. They understood at last the purpose of the Child lying helpless in the manger at Bethlehem, dependent on the care of a mother and a foster-father, flying in fear from his enemies; of the Boy growing up among other boys, "in wisdom, and age, and grace before God and men," at Nazareth, and plying a carpenter's trade; of the Man standing as a sinner among sinners at the Jordan, on that memorable day when they first met him, waiting his turn to be baptized by John.

They knew at last why, like other men, even more than other men, he underwent the fire of temptation; why

[65] Heb. 7:26.

he hungered and thirsted, and endured fatigue of body, and was weary and slept. They knew why he showed so simply the affections of his sensitive nature: sympathy for suffering on one side, indignation with injustice on another; tenderness at one time with weak human nature, at another, firmness stern and unflinching; love of friends and denunciation of enemies; childlike expression alike of joy and pain, of gratitude and of disappointment; overflowing thanks when men gave him cause for consolation, grief unto tears in face of loss. Even after he had died, and had risen again, they saw why and how he had been so eager that his own should recognize him once again for what he was, truly man, and not a disembodied spirit; letting them embrace his feet,[66] speaking with a plaintive voice that could not be mistaken,[67] eating before them, bidding them to handle him,[68] coming down to any condition they might lay down in order that they might be convinced.[69]

In another way, again, now that all was over, they saw the complete and perfect human nature of Jesus manifested. It was in his full submission to God the Father. The

[66] Matt. 28:9.
[67] John 20:16.
[68] Luke 24:29-43.
[69] John 20:27.

will of the Father — that was for him the beginning and the end. To carry out that will was his life's work; to preach his commission was his allotted task.[70] The mind of the Father was above all things else; the wish of the Father was the final goal.[71] He would seek no glory but such as should redound to the glory of the Father;[72] upon the Father he would lean and depend for everything. With the Father he would constantly unite himself in prayer,[73] thanking him alike in joy and in sorrow,[74] when things were hard appealing to him,[75] often for his miracles seeking his assistance.[76] In all, the story of the end submission of the real human will of Jesus to the will of the Father in heaven is continually repeated, from the prayer against his own petition in the Garden[77] until on Calvary are heard first the cry of desolation,[78] then the last word of all,

[70] John 5:19; 8:28.

[71] Matt. 24:36, 39.

[72] Mark 5:19; John 8:49 (RSV = John 8:50); 14:13.

[73] Luke 6:12; 9:18, 28; Matt. 14:23.

[74] Luke 10:21; John 11:1-46.

[75] John 12:27.

[76] Mark 7:34; John 11:38, 41.

[77] Matt. 16:39.

[78] Matt. 27:46.

with which in fullest confidence he gives his soul into his Father's keeping.[79]

Without any doubt, therefore, Jesus had impressed upon those who had lived most intimately with him the fact of his human limitations. So much was he a child to his mother that she could never speak to him nor treat him as other than her own son: complaining to him when he did what she could not understand;[80] putting the needs of others before him;[81] seeking him out when trouble threatened him;[82] when he died, claiming a mother's place by his suffering body.[83] Neighbors had known him only as the carpenter of Nazareth, and the impression never left them. His fellow-villagers despised him because he was just that, and therefore could not be more.[84] Publicans and sinners could presume so much upon their acquaintance with him as to invite him to sit with them at table;[85] women realized his needs and were glad to follow him and

[79] Luke 23:46.
[80] Luke 2:48.
[81] John 2:3.
[82] Matt. 12:19.
[83] John 19:25.
[84] Luke 4:16-30.
[85] Matt. 9:9-17.

help him.[86] Crowds could knock up against him in the streets;[87] could hold him hemmed in among them so that he must needs be rescued from them;[88] when he said what seemed to them absurd could openly jeer before him.[89] Friends could blame him when he let himself be hustled to and fro, and say he was becoming mad;[90] could warn him against impending danger which his seeming imprudence provoked;[91] could contradict him to his face;[92] even when he was transfigured before them, could come to themselves and discover that, after all, he was "only Jesus."[93] They could wrangle in his company, forgetting he was there;[94] they could offer him wise counsel as to what he ought to do;[95] they could take it upon themselves to decide who should come near him and who should not;[96] in

---

[86] Luke 8:1-3.

[87] Mark 5:31.

[88] Mark 3:21.

[89] Matt. 9:24.

[90] Mark 3:21.

[91] Matt. 15:12.

[92] Matt. 6:22.

[93] Matt. 17:8.

[94] Mark 9:33.

[95] John 7:3-4.

[96] Matt. 19:13; 20:31.

his very presence, they could complain of those who honored him in ways which he accepted, but which did not suit their fancy.[97] If intimacy and familiarity may prove how completely Jesus was a man among men, then on every page of the Gospels we have the evidence in abundance.

∞

The witness of Jesus' friends

To men living so intimately with him, especially to those with whom he dwelt habitually, at whose board he ate, by whose side he slept in their cottages upon the floors, whom he kept with him in all his journeys, it was inevitable that, as man, he should be well known. What, then, is the account they give of him? We are often told, "No man is a hero to his valet," and by that we are given to understand that familiarity discovers weaknesses even in a hero. Yet what do we learn from the intimates of Jesus Christ?

From the day when the sinless John the Baptist acknowledges him to be far more sinless than himself,[98] and pointed him out to all as the spotless Lamb of God, who would take away the sin of the world,[99] there is never the

[97] Matt. 26:8.
[98] Matt. 3:17.
[99] John 1:36.

slightest deviation. Simon, a year later, shows the impression that has deepened in him when he cries, "Depart from me, for I am a sinful man, O Lord."[100] And on that occasion, as on so many others, he spoke for the handful of men who had reason to know him best. He chose them apart from all others, and they clung closely to him; he gave them himself as an example, and as such, they studied him in every detail; he called them his brothers and sisters, and they were beside themselves with joy. They do his work for him; they are tested concerning their fidelity; others may abandon him, but again Simon sums up the impression of them all: "Lord, to whom shall we go? Thou hast the words of eternal life."[101]

A little later, and it has grown deeper; once more Simon speaks for his companions. "Thou art the Christ, the Son of the living God."[102] It is the height of their confession of faith, but it is founded on their knowledge of the perfection of the man of whom they spoke. And there were deeper things to follow; from henceforth they studied him more closely as the model for their lives. "Come to me" had now grown into "Learn of me," and

[100] Luke 5:8.
[101] John 6:69 (RSV = John 6:68).
[102] Matt. 16:16.

they felt the justice of the claim. They saw his infinite forgiveness and asked how many times they were to forgive.[103] They watched him often in prayer and asked that they might be taught to do the same.[104] He told them to forgive as they themselves would wish to be forgiven; by word he taught them that which he could not teach them by example.

The nearer he comes to the end, the more are they compelled to remark on the two striking features of his life: on the one hand, his bold condemnation of evildoers; on the other, his never-ceasing sympathy for the weak, the sinful, the downtrodden, and the contemned. They say very little; after the confession of Peter at Caesarea, less than others do the Apostles express their feelings and beliefs; but the impression is unmistakable: their Master is the Master indeed, who had the word of God, was the beloved of God, and taught more by example than by precept, and who, by his utter truth, won all to himself. He was wholly true, he was wholly to be trusted, he was wholly worthy to be loved: "Lord, thou knowest that I love thee."[105]

[103] Matt. 18:21.
[104] Luke 11:1.
[105] John 21:16.

The Good Galilean

But if the Apostles said little, there were others about them both more voluble and more demonstrative, and the Evangelists quote their words and describe their actions with evident approval and delight. In every case, it is the homage paid to the utter genuineness of their Master that delights them. The learned Pharisee Nicodemus knew to whom he was speaking when he said, "Rabbi, we know that thou art come a teacher from God."[106] No less did that poor woman of Samaria, a little later, a creature at the opposite extreme, who, after one conversation, could go away and say, "Is not this the Christ?"[107] The Roman soldier in Capernaum had learned much of this Jew before he could submit to pray, "Lord, I am not worthy that thou shouldst enter under my roof," as well as the woman, the sinner in the city, before, without any conditions, she could lay at his feet the whole of her miserable burden.[108] When the multitude cried out with enthusiasm, "He hath done all things well,"[109] clearly they spoke of more than miracles; it was more than miracles that made the common people of Jerusalem say to one another in the streets,

[106] John 3:2.
[107] John 4:29.
[108] Matt. 8:15; Luke 7:36-50.
[109] Mark 7:37.

"He is a good man"[110]and use this as an answer to his enemies, who tried to seduce them.

So we may go on; as the clouds thicken, the Light of the world seems only to become more manifest. The mother's heart that cried out in the crowd, "Blessed is the womb that bore thee"[111] proclaimed what a good mother's instinct is quick to discern; so, too, was it with the ever-growing believers in Judea, who, in response to the abuse of his enemies, fell back on the evidence of the Baptist, confirmed by what they themselves had seen: "John, indeed, did no sign, but all things whatsoever John said of this man were true."[112] The children who ran to him and clung about him on the road up from Perea, and the mothers who so easily committed them to his care,[113] the women who gladly entertained him in their homes,[114] the young men fired at the sight of him to be themselves great and true and noble,[115] the publicans and sinners, men who had accepted their fate, but who needed from him no

[110]John 7:12.
[111]Luke 11:27.
[112]John 10:41-42.
[113]Matt. 19:10-15.
[114]Luke 10:38.
[115]Matt. 19:16; 20:20.

The Good Galilean

more than a look or a word to find their whole lives changed[116] — all these and more, coming from so many varied angles, are witnesses more eloquent than any declarations of the crystal clearness of his life.

At the end of all, this is made only the more conspicuous. When remorse compels his betrayer to confess, in the sight of his destroyers, "I have sinned in betraying innocent blood,"[117] they cannot contradict him; tacitly they confess that what he says is true. When the wife of Pilate warns the Roman governor, "Have thou nothing to do with this just man";[118] when Pilate himself, in feeble self-defense, declares, "I am innocent of the blood of this just man";[119] when, on the cross, the criminal hanging by his side defends him with the words: "This man hath done no evil";[120] when, after he is dead, the guard beneath the gibbet sums up all he has witnessed in the sentence: "Indeed this was a just man";[121] we know something of the minds of those about him at the moment when, of all

[116]Luke 19:1-10.
[117]Matt. 27:4.
[118]Matt. 27:19.
[119]Matt. 27:24.
[120]Luke 23:41.
[121]Luke 23:47.

times in his life, it was most essential that he should be thought guilty.

Hence it was that after he had left this earth, when Peter, for the first time, stood before the people of Jerusalem to give his witness, it was natural and easy for him to speak to them of Jesus as "the Holy One and the Just";[122] it was natural for him, before such an audience, to sum up his life in the single phrase: "Jesus of Nazareth: how God anointed him with the Holy Ghost and with power, who went about doing good."[123] When later he wrote to his neophytes, he could best describe him so: "Who did no sin, neither was guile found in his mouth. Who, when he was reviled, did not revile: when he suffered, he threatened not, but delivered himself to him that judged him unjustly. Who his own self bore our sins in his body upon the tree." And again: "Christ died once for our sins, the just for the unjust."[124]

Precisely the same is the evidence of the other Apostles; they dwell, not upon his wonder-working, not upon his preaching, but upon the surpassing, positive sinlessness of Jesus. Thus, St. John sums up his Master and his

[122] Acts 3:14.
[123] Acts 10:38.
[124] 1 Pet. 2:22-24; 3:18.

work: "You know that he appeared to take away our sins, and in him there is no sin. Whosoever abideth in him sinneth not; and whosoever sinneth hath not seen him nor known him."[125] The same he puts elsewhere in another form: "My little children, these things I write to you that you may not sin. But if any man sin, we have an advocate with the Father, Jesus Christ the just."[126] So much does the disciple whom Jesus loved make of the spotless innocence of his Beloved. And akin to it is the single sentence of St. James, the "brother of the Lord": "You have condemned and put to death the just One: and he resisted you not."[127]

∾

The witness of Jesus' enemies

All this and more we have from those who were Jesus' friends, who were won by him, or at least were not disposed to stand against him. But there were other eyes than those turned upon him: eyes that looked, not merely for any flaw in word or deed, but for any pretext whatsoever, for any show of evidence, whether true or false, that might

[125] 1 John 3:5.
[126] 1 John 2:1.
[127] Jas. 5:6.

be turned to his destruction. We find them first in Judea, their suspicions roused and their machinations working before he has yet begun to move.[128] We find them next in Galilee, early in his public life, combining with Herodians, whom otherwise they would have scorned to know.[129] Later, in Judea, Pharisees and Sadducees join hands to catch him in any way they can. In the streets of Jerusalem, after their manner, in the hearing of the people, they boldly say, "Thou hast a devil" and "We know that this man is a sinner"; but when they are asked to specify their charge, it is shamefully little that they can rake together. Three times at least Jesus challenged them to frame an accusation. "Why seek you to kill me?" he asked them in the Temple court at the last Feast of Tabernacles, and a little later, "Which of you shall accuse me of sin?" Again, in the same place at the Feast of Dedication, only four months before his death: "Many good works I have showed you from my Father. For which of those works do you stone me?"[130]

In the Garden of Gethsemane, when at last they seized him, there is more than rebuke; there is overwhelming evidence in his favor that could not be denied in his simple

[128] John 4:1.
[129] Mark 3:6.
[130] John 7:20; 8:46; 9:24; 10:32.

words: "Are ye come out as it were against a thief with swords and clubs? When I was daily with you in the Temple, you did not stretch forth your hands against me."[131]

In spite of these searching eyes kept incessantly upon him from the beginning to the end of his career, and in spite of the challenge with which he confronted them, what did these experts in duplicity find?

• "What sign dost thou show, seeing thou dost these things?"[132]

• "Therefore did the Jews persecute Jesus because he did these things on the Sabbath."[133]

• "Is not this the son of Joseph? And his mother, do we not know her?"[134]

• "He blasphemeth. Who can forgive sins but God only?"[135]

• "Why doth your master eat with publicans and sinners?"[136]

[131] Luke 22:52-53.
[132] John 2:18.
[133] John 5:16.
[134] Luke 4:22.
[135] Mark 2:7.
[136] Matt. 9:11.

• "This man, if he were a prophet, would know surely who and what manner of woman this is that toucheth him, that she is a sinner."[137]

• "This man casteth not out devils but by Beelzebub, the prince of the devils."[138]

• "How came this man by all these things? Is not this the carpenter, the son of Mary?"[139]

• "How can this man give us his flesh to eat?"[140]

• "Thou hast a devil."[141]

• "We know this man whence he is: but when the Christ cometh, no man knoweth whence he is."[142]

• "Doth the Christ come out of Galilee?"[143]

• "Search the Scriptures and see that out of Galilee a prophet riseth not."[144]

[137] Luke 7:39.
[138] Matt. 12:24.
[139] Mark 6:23.
[140] John 6:53 (RSV = John 6:52).
[141] John 7:20.
[142] John 7:27.
[143] John 7:4.
[144] John 7:52.

• "Thou givest testimony of thyself; thy testimony is not true."[145]

• "Do not we say well that thou art a Samaritan, and hast a devil?"[146]

• "Now we know that thou hast a devil."[147]

• "This man is not of God, who keepeth not the Sabbath."[148]

• "We know that this man is a sinner."[149]

• "We know that God spoke to Moses, but as to this man, we know not whence he is."[150]

• "He hath a devil and is mad. Why hear you him?"[151]

• "For a good work we stone thee not, but for blasphemy; and because that thou, being a man, makest thyself God."[152]

[145] John 8:13.
[146] John 8:48.
[147] John 8:52.
[148] John 9:16.
[149] John 9:24.
[150] John 9:29.
[151] John 10:20.
[152] John 10:33.

- "What do we, for this man doth many miracles?"[153]

- "It is expedient for you that one man should die for the people, and that the whole nation perish not."[154]

- "Do you see that we prevail nothing? Behold the whole world is gone after him."[155]

The series wearies us. His enemies themselves were weary of this vain repetition of empty phrases. On the last day of his public teaching they were compelled to change their tactics.

"And they sent to him their disciples, with the Herodians, saying, 'Master, we know that thou art a true speaker, and teachest the way of God in truth. Neither carest thou for any man, for thou dost not regard the person of man.' "[156]

It is no wonder, then, that at the end, when at last they have him at their mercy, they must deliberately seek false witness, they must deliberately garble and twist his words, that they may have wherewith to accuse him even among themselves.[157] Before others they must conclude

[153] John 11:47.
[154] John 11:50.
[155] John 12:19.
[156] Matt. 22:15.
[157] Mark 14:55.

with assumptions they could never attempt to prove: "If he were not a malefactor, we would not have delivered him up to thee";[158] and after Jesus was dead and buried, and as it seemed could no longer speak, they must still emit their slander: "That seducer."[159]

This, then, was all. Never before or since has any man been subjected to so keen a scrutiny; never has hatred been so watchful, so determined to destroy; and yet this was all. Any trifle would have sufficed, an imprudent word however true, a hasty deed however justified, a look, a gesture that could have indicated a hard or bitter mind; yet not so much as a trifle could be found. Jesus Christ! Weighed in the balance and found perfect, tried in the severest furnace and found to be purest gold!

∞

Jesus' witness of himself

But now, upon all this, we have a further evidence, which at once puts Jesus on another plane from that of other men. It is the witness he gives of himself. Whatever else he was, on the evidence alike of friends and enemies, he was true, he was sincere, he was transparently genuine;

[158] John 18:30.
[159] Matt. 27:63.

indeed, it was his utter genuineness that in the end was the final proof to his friends; to his enemies was their despair. As, then, with others who are true, when he speaks of himself, he must be heard.

And what does he say? Other men and women have been holy; a few by the grace of God have been preserved in simple innocence from childhood to old age, and on that account alone have been treasured as the jewels of our race; but no man, save only Jesus Christ, has dared to claim holiness and innocence as belonging to himself from his very nature. No saint, however confirmed in grace, has ever ceased to own himself a sinner, or to be in constant fear of his own rejection. "I chastise my body," says St. Paul, "and bring it into subjection, lest while preaching to others I myself may become a castaway."[160]

And more pertinently, St. John: "If we say that we have no sin, we deceive ourselves, and the truth is not in us."[161] Very differently, as we have seen, does the same saint speak of Jesus Christ: "If we confess our sins, he is faithful and just, to forgive us our sins, and to cleanse us from all iniquity."[162] And when he so emphatically marks

[160] 1 Cor. 9:27.
[161] 1 John 1:8.
[162] 1 John 1:9.

the contrast, he does but repeat that which Jesus, again and again, implicitly at least declared of himself. He came to the Jordan and was baptized with sinners, but not until he who baptized him had expressly proclaimed him to be more sinless than himself.[163] He ate and drank with, and permitted himself to be called the friend of publicans and sinners, but never did he allow, and never did they pretend, that he was one of them.[164] He taught men to pray that they might have their sins forgiven; but it was always in the second person; never did he unite himself with them in that petition. For them he said, "Thus, therefore, shall you pray . . . 'Forgive us our trespasses,' " and in that he included all men; but for himself, "Father, the hour is come . . . I have glorified thee on the earth. I have finished the work which thou gavest me to do. And now glorify thou me, O Father, with thyself."[165]

So in practice does he make a sharp distinction between himself and other men. But he does it also explicitly. In the Sermon on the Mount, in very marked words, he speaks to his hearers: "If you, being evil, know how to give good gifts to your children . . ." carefully separating them

[163]Matt. 3:14.
[164]Matt. 9:10.
[165]John 17:4-5.

from himself.[166] By the well of Samaria, he says to his disciples, "My meat is to do the will of him that sent me,"[167] a first lesson in their understanding of him.

Before the Jews in the Temple he is most emphatic:

• "He that speaketh of himself seeketh his own glory: but he that seeketh the glory of him that sent him, he is true and there is no injustice in him."[168]

• "He that sent me is with me; and he hath not left me alone. For I do always the things that please him."[169]

• "Which of you shall convince me of sin? If I say the truth to you, why do you not believe me?"[170]

• "If I glorify myself, my glory is nothing. It is my Father that glorifieth me, of whom you say that he is your God. And you have not known him, but I know him. And if I say that I know him not, I shall be like to you, a liar. But I do know him and do keep his word."[171]

[166] Matt. 7:11.
[167] John 4:34.
[168] John 7:18.
[169] John 8:29.
[170] John 8:46.
[171] John 8:54-55.

- "If I do not the works of my Father, believe me not. But if I do, though you will not believe me, believe the works: that you may know and believe that the Father is me and I in the Father."[172]

Add to this his words in the Supper room: "The prince of this world cometh, and in me he hath not anything."[173]

So he speaks of himself, but his actions are yet more eloquent. In his attitude to evil of any kind, he assumes a position that only he who is conscious of being its absolute master could assume. His very name has this significance; it is given because "he will save his people from their sins."[174] He is first announced by the Baptist as "the Lamb of God, who taketh away the sin of the world,"[175] as, just before, he had been declared from heaven to be one in whom God "was well pleased."[176] From the first, he is the avowed enemy of sin, who will drive it always before him, will conquer its kingdom, will bid its master begone;[177]

[172] John 10:37-38.
[173] John 14:30.
[174] Matt. 1:21.
[175] John 1:29.
[176] Matt. 3:17.
[177] Matt. 4:10.

never for an instant will he be subject to it or fear it. In whatever form it appears, he denounces and defies it;[178] in his own name he lays down fresh standards concerning it: "I say to you . . ."[179]

On the other hand, when the guilty soul comes penitent before him, Jesus forgives as by his own right[180] — nay, more, he hands on to others the power to forgive sins in his own name. Devils declare his independence of them: "What have we to do with thee, thou Holy One of God?"[181] They cringe before him and appeal to him, as to one who is wholly their Lord.[182] John had described him as one whose wand would be in his hand, and who would sift the chaff from the grain;[183] he himself declares that he is the judge of sinners; he will reward and he will punish.[184]

As the end draws near, the claim grows ever more prominent. His last days witness, as it were, a struggle in his soul

[178] Mark 3:28.
[179] Matt. 5:18.
[180] Matt. 9:2; Luke 7:48; John 8:11.
[181] Mark 1:24.
[182] Mark 5:10.
[183] Matt. 3:12.
[184] Matt. 25:31, 46.

between justice and mercy toward those who offended his Father, but for himself there is never a shadow of doubt or fear or apprehension. In the Garden, he takes upon himself the iniquity of us all; for man he is "made sin," and, as such, he suffers.

When at last he comes to die, he does not, like other men, pray for forgiveness; he prays only that others may be forgiven: "Father, forgive them, for they know not what they do."[185] In him there is no repentance; for him, that would be untrue; instead, when another repents, even from the cross, he exercises his prerogative: "Amen, I say to thee, this day thou shalt be with me in paradise."[186] There is desolation, but there is no remorse in the cry: "My God, my God, why hast thou forsaken me?"[187] It is answered by the last word of all: "Father, into thy hands I commend my spirit."[188]

Note: This is not the place in which to discuss at length the question of the sanctity of Christ. For clearly,

[185] Luke 23:34.
[186] Luke 23:43.
[187] Matt. 27:46.
[188] Luke 23:46.

when we speak of his sanctity, we speak of that which belongs to him as God as well as man; and here we are concerned with that which belongs to him as man alone, as the model of manhood. We have seen that he did not sin; we might go on to show — were we studying him in all his perfection, we should go on to show — that he was incapable of sinning: "Holy, innocent, undefiled, separated from sinners."[189]

Nor would that be all. It would remain to be shown that in virtue of the union of the human soul of Jesus with the Word of God, sanctity, holiness came to him as of his very nature; he was not only sanctified by grace, as other men are sanctified; he was sanctified as being the incarnate Son of God: "The holy one which shall be born of thee shall be called the Son of God."[190]

Still, there is the more human aspect that we may not omit. If Jesus was made "in all things like to man without sin," then was he like to man in the possession of sanctifying grace. "And the Word was made flesh, and dwelt amongst us . . . full of grace and truth," says St. John;[191] and this would seem to be the meaning of many

[189] Heb. 7:26.
[190] Luke 1:35.
[191] John 1:14.

The Good Galilean

passages in the first teaching of the Apostles.[192] This explains to us the meaning of St. Luke when he says: "And Jesus advanced in wisdom and age and grace with God and men."[193]

---

[192] Cf. Acts 10:38.
[193] Luke 2:52.

Chapter 3

∞

Jesus Is a Model of Love for Others

"And it came to pass when Jesus had fully ended these words, the people were in admiration at his doctrine. For he was teaching them as one having power, and not as the scribes and Pharisees."[194]

There are points in the story of the Gospels when the figure in the center seems to rise out from its surroundings; when the reader's vision expands; when, in that vision, that central figure seems to occupy at once, not only all that period of years during which it lived, but the whole of this world's history: "Jesus Christ, yesterday, and today, and the same forever."[195]

At one of these points, in a summary such as this, we may do best to study him. Although in consequence many

[194]Matt. 7:28-29.
[195]Heb. 13:8.

61

other details may be lost, although we may miss that variety, and universality, and all-embracing sympathy of soul which the whole story portrays, still by so doing, we may hope to catch the more essential details, from which we may judge of the rest.

Such a point we have at the conclusion of the Sermon on the Mount. It is comparatively early in Jesus' public life. Hitherto he has confined himself, for the most part, in and about Capernaum. By generosity overflowing, he has won the hearts of the people; by personal contact, he has stirred the enthusiasm of his disciples; now the moment has come for the more formal opening of the kingdom.

For an hour or more that morning, on the mountainside that runs up behind the little town, Jesus has been speaking and the people have listened; they have listened in silence, and the fascination of his words has carried them out of themselves. For an hour or more, that single voice has been pouring itself out, and has lifted them above their sordid surroundings, into a world where sorrow has been turned into blessedness;[196] has given them new joy and courage in the good tidings that, after all, they are of some account in the eyes of their Father;[197] has freed them

[196] Matt. 5:3 ff.
[197] Matt. 5:16.

from the bondage of the Law, making it a glory to brave things yet harder than the Law had ever enjoined; has given them a new understanding of sin, until innocence, truth, simplicity, forgiveness, loving-kindness, and charity have shone out as the real honor of mankind; has given the noblest possible ideal for life and character, even the ideal of the Father, God himself: "Be you therefore perfect, as your heavenly Father is perfect"; has taught them to pray, to speak to that Father, in terms that can never be forgotten; has cut through all hypocrisy and brought to perfect light the genuine truth of the soul; has shown them where absolute confidence can reach, higher than the flight of the birds of the air, lower than the grass beneath their feet; has defined and vindicated true justice, which is also mercy, equality, and meekness; and although what has been said has ended on a note of warning, still has it been with joy, and hope, and love unutterable in the air.[198]

He has said all this, and he has said it in their own language. Never once has he needed to go beyond their own vocabulary, the vocabulary of that Galilean countryside, their own ideas, their own surroundings, to teach and to illustrate his teaching; they have caught and understood

[198]Matt. 5:21, 44, 48; 6:9, 16, 26; 7:1, 24.

every word. As on a former occasion, speaking to poor working men at their street corner, he had made use of their patched clothing, their bottles and their wine, to bring home to them the truth of the Kingdom,[199] so now he has caught hold of the things about him and them by which to teach them the word. He speaks of their every-day joys and sorrows; the salt of their everyday meal; the village perched up there on the hill above them; the candle-stick in the windowsill; their daily conversation with its oaths and loose language; their daily bickerings before the local judge; their household quarrels; the local thief; the local borrower of money; the sun now beating down upon them; the rain, which had but recently ceased for the season; the pompous display of religion in the streets; their daily toil and their daily wages, carefully stored and hidden away in their money-bags at home; the rust and the moth, which were a constant trouble; the raven at that moment hovering above them; the flowers flourishing abundantly around them; the green grass on the plain with all its rich promise; their food, their drink, their clothing, their need of daily sustenance; the ditch over there between the fields; their dogs; their swine; their fish and their eggs; the stones on the hillside, with the danger

[199] Matt. 9:16.

of snakes and scorpions beneath them; the gate in the wall hard by; their sheep and the wolves they knew only too well; their vines and their fig trees; their thorns and thistles; their fruit trees, good and bad; their house of detention; last, down there below on the lakeside, a cottage that has fallen to ruins in a storm, and another that stands secure.[200]

∞

Jesus' words appeal to all

He has spoken to them in their own language. He has said what he has said in the language of their lives. He has seen them in their poverty. He has seen them broken and weighed down by cruelty and injustice and misunderstanding, and has blessed them for it all; he has blessed them for it and has poured soothing oil into their wounds. He has listened to them in their heated quarrels, a brother against a brother, and has given them the means of reconciliation. He has noticed their proneness to coarse vices and has forewarned them; he has heard their loose talk, their ribald oaths, their cursing that has led to other abuses, their rising hatred one of another with revenge to

[200] Matt. 5:3, 13-15, 22, 25, 33, 42, 45; 6:2, 19, 20, 28, 30-31; 7:6, 9, 13-14, 16, 19, 23-24; Luke 6:39; 12:24.

follow as an imagined duty, and has pulled them up with a word that has swept all rancor aside.[201] He has watched them at their prayer, in their almsgiving, during the fasting season, and has warned them against mere outward show. He has compassionated with them in their daily cares, their anxiety for their daily bread and their daily clothing, their eagerness to hoard their daily earnings, their eyes keenly watching the tradesman's scales in the bazaar, and has boldly and assuringly lifted them above it all.[202] He has weighed the love of father and son, of friend and neighbor, and has accurately gauged how far they can be tried. He has gazed on the good workman and the negligent, and has judged the value of their work.[203] He has lived their lives, he is one of them, he knows them through and through, their good points and their bad points, and he loves them; in spite of all, he loves them and gives them all this.

And yet, on the other side, while he remains but one among them, how much above not only them but all others does he claim to be! With an assurance such as no man — not even any prophet before him — had ever ventured

[201] Matt. 5:11, 22, 28, 37.
[202] Matt. 6:3, 33.
[203] Matt. 7:11, 26.

to assume, he pronounces blessing upon them; with the might of a monarch he pronounces woe on others.[204]

He speaks as of his own authority: "I am come to fulfill"; "I tell you"; "I say to you."[205] Who is this who so speaks of himself? He quotes Moses and the prophets, and sets up himself and his new doctrine as something that shall transcend them all.[206] He gives them commands beyond those of the Law, boldly contradicting those of scribes and Pharisees,[207] yet promises rewards of which neither Law nor Pharisees have ever dreamed: "Your reward shall be great"; "You shall be the children of the Father"; "Your heavenly Father shall repay you."[208]

He takes it upon himself to teach all men how to pray, how to commune with Almighty God, and God he boldly calls his own Father and theirs. He speaks of this Father as of one with whom he is personally familiar; tells them of his providence and care for them as of something with which he is intimate, of his mercy as of a characteristic trait, of his perfection as an ideal toward which they

[204] Luke 6:22, 24.
[205] Matt. 5:17, 20, 22.
[206] Matt. 5:19.
[207] Matt. 5:20.
[208] Matt. 5:12, 45; 6:4.

themselves, being sons, might hope to aspire. He speaks of the kingdom of heaven as if it were his own, promises it to whom he will. Strange things indeed he adds about the value of his word and the keeping of it, as if the very being of men and of the world depended on it.[209]

Still with it all there has been no arrogance, no sense of false assumption, not a single word that has not rung true; assurance, yes, and certainty, and dignity, and grandeur of ideal, but no arrogance. Truth has sounded in every word he has said — human truth, the truth that lies at the root of all that is best in man, to which the heart of man instantly responds; bravery in face of trial; moral courage to its last extreme,[210] which has sent a thrill of honor and glory tingling through the veins of all who have heard him; at the same time a lowliness, a submissiveness, a contentment, a joy in whatever might befall, which has made the most crushed life noble. And with it has gone a gentleness of touch upon the most sensitive of suffering, a compassion that has entered into, and condoned, and lifted up, and made bright again the most downcast and the most sinful; an understanding of the love of friend and enemy, and the extremes to which it would venture; a love of

[209] Matt. 5:48; 7:20, 23.
[210] Matt. 5:11, 44.

the Father, an unquestioning surrender to the Father, a familiar dealing with the Father as became a well-loved son, a simple reliance on the Father, tender and human as that of any child, even while he sat there master of them all, strong and adamant.

Thus, inevitably from the words he said did these people come to gaze at and think upon the man who said them. All gazed at him; all alike were drawn to him; none of any kind were omitted. The little children gazed open-mouthed, and under the spell forgot their mothers, whose arms were around them;[211] the mothers gazed and for the time forgot their children. Old age bent double, leaning on its stick, looked up at him where he sat upon his stone and was stirred to new life;[212] youth with its dreams looked, and was fascinated, and longed to do great things.[213] Ignorance and stupidity listened and rejoiced that it heard what it could understand; learning and cleverness listened and was weighed down with the burden of thought that it bore away.[214] Men in high station came, with intent to test him, and stood before him paralyzed, feeling the

[211] Cf. Matt. 19:13.
[212] Cf. Luke 13:11.
[213] Cf. Matt. 10:17.
[214] Cf. Matt. 13:11; 19:10.

force of his every word; crawling men of low degree and stricken down sat on the edge of the crowd, and knew no less that the message was for them.[215] Innocent, true souls were there, and came away rejoicing, spurred to yet more truth of life and sacrifice.[216] Guilty souls, shameless hearts felt their guilt the more, yet through it all were able to brush away the tears of despair, and look up with hope such as they had never known before, and love revived within them, the love that came out from and went back to that man.[217]

∞

Jesus' listeners long to know him fully

Who was he? What was he? What should they think of him? How should they describe him to themselves? What portrait of him should they bear away, stamped upon their hearts? They gazed and gazed, speechless and entranced, longing to enter into his soul.

They saw the fire of zeal flashing from his eyes, flying from his words like sparks from iron, yet never a shadow fell upon the patience, the patience without limit, revealed in

[215]Cf. Luke 10:37; 14:25.
[216]Cf. Matt. 20:21.
[217]Cf. Luke 15:1.

his face. They bowed before the grandeur, the nobility, the fervor for the truth, and for all that was best in men, yet they recognized the lenient condoning, the gentle indulgence and compassion where they failed. They felt the holiness, the earnestness, the seriousness of purpose that compelled to silence, yet with it all was there a brightness, a gaiety of heart, a cheerful vision, a pouring out of blessing and reward that made all life a sheer joy. They were awed by his extolling of prayer, and of self-surrender, as if nothing else were of moment, yet alongside was a knowledge of the active things of life that only experience could have taught. They were lifted up by the sight of a greatness of soul, and of outlook, and of ideal, and of endeavor that might have paralyzed them, were it not for the deep lowliness and union with them, every one, that made them feel he was their servant even while he was their Master; and along with him all things were possible; they could do all things in him who strengthened them.[218]

They looked at him and they saw much that lay beneath. There was determination that never looked aside, that never for a moment flinched or hesitated, never bent or swerved, pressing on to a goal straight before it; yet was it ever gentle, ever considerate, ever forbearing, taking poor

[218]Matt. 19:26; Phil. 4:13.

71

weakness by the hand, lifting up the fallen, carrying the cripple on its shoulder.

There was energy, action, daring to rush forward that carried all before it, yet nonetheless never losing self-control, always composed, always at peace within itself, a sense of quiet reigning all around it. There was hatred of everything evil, indignation, wrath, condemnation fire, and death — death undying, meted out in fierce anger against it; yet never did a sinner feel himself condemned or his hope extinguished, but only knew that forgiveness, love, and warm pressure to a warm heart awaited him if he would have it. There was a keen sense of justice — justice idealized, justice defended, strict justice without favor; yet was the hand that dealt it out soft and tender and soothing. There was passionate love of truth — truth that feared nothing, truth open and outspoken, to saint and sinner, to selfish rich and to sensitive poor, to men in high places and to those downtrodden; yet for them all, an attraction none of them could resist, a sincerity that forestalled opposition or resentment.

He was tolerant and he was stern. He bent to the weakest, yet he stood up like a tower; he yielded, yet he held his own. He was a mountain of strength, yet a mother could not be more gentle. He was lost like a child in the arms of his Father, yet was he ever fully conscious and master of himself. All this was uttered in every word he spoke, was expressed in every look and gesture.

Who was this man? What was he? They longed to know him more, and they did not know that the longing within them was the firstfruit of love.

For indeed, throughout his address, love and love only had spoken all the time. Nothing else could have given such insight into the souls of other men; nothing else could have fostered so great a craving to bless, and to give, and to receive back, and to make secure. There was love for the poor, for the meek and lowly, for the sorrowful; love for the hungry of heart, for the merciful of heart, for the clean of heart; love for the makers of peace, and for those who failed to make peace and therefore endured persecution; love, on the other side, for the rich, and the happy, and the contented, warning them against false security; love for them all, both the motley crowd before him, and the chosen Twelve who stood around the throne where he sat. Indeed, for these last, he had special affection; they were his own, the salt of the earth, the light of the world,[219] the Apostles that were to be. For them in particular he had come; he had chosen them, he was living for them, soon he would die for them, and for them

219 Matt. 5:12, 13.

The Good Galilean

would rise again from the dead. With them he would always abide, with them and with all who would have him, the Lover of each, longing for each, speaking to each the same winning words he had just spoken on that mountainside, the bosom friend of every hungry soul and its complete satisfaction, if only it would come up the hill and look for him, and find him, and listen to him, and lose its heart to him, as he had already lost his own to it.

In the light of all that came after, it is not too much to say that this was the Jesus Christ men saw as he spoke to them on the mountainside. "And it came to pass when Jesus had fully ended these words, the people were in admiration at his doctrine. For he was teaching them as one having power, and not as the scribes and Pharisees."

Chapter 4

Jesus Is an Example of Every Perfection

In the last chapter, we were content to look at Jesus Christ as he reveals himself in but one scene of his life. To complete the picture, and to prove its entire consistency, it would be necessary to go through all the Gospels, and to draw out each chapter in at least the same detail. But this would be a work of many volumes; nay, as St. John says, "the whole world would not be able to contain the books that should be written."[220]

But, instead, can we bring together our impressions of this model of perfect man, so as to distinguish him from other men? Can we say what are his special, individual features? We cannot. Intensely individual as he is, easily known and recognized, nevertheless, as has been said, the more we try to fix him down, to appoint limitations, to

[220] John 21:25.

declare him to be this and not that, so much the more does he elude us. On the other hand, the more we appreciate and see, the more he grows upon us, until any description of him seems a mere shadow of the truth, wholly inadequate.

For how shall we define him? We watch him from the beginning coming down from Nazareth to the Jordan, one among a multitude, differing from none; or if there is a difference, it has been only this: that he has been so like, not simply to all men in general, but to every man with whom he has come into contact. From that moment to the end on Calvary, he has never lost this equality. His office of preacher has not destroyed it; his working of wonders has not set him on a pedestal apart. Whatever men, in moments of enthusiasm, have said of him, they have never been able to resist this intimate union and equality of Jesus Christ with every man he has met. They have been struck with awe, yet have they remained familiar; they have proclaimed him a prophet, "the prophet," and have wished to make him their king, yet they have continued to press upon him in their streets; they have called him the Son of God, and almost in the same breath, when he spoke, they have contradicted and corrected him.[221]

[221] Mark 8:32.

Jesus Is an Example of Every Perfection

Nevertheless, by a strange paradox, as the life expands, it grows upon us that in one thing at least he has differed from others; nay, in this one point, he has claimed for himself an abiding difference. No matter how otherwise he has been weak and has been humbled in body and in soul like other men, no matter how much he has been tempted, yet never could friend or enemy, when it occurred to them to search, find in him anything that so much as partook of the nature of an evil deed. He has known sin and its dread significance as other men have not known it; he has hated it as other men could never hate it; he has set himself to destroy it, to "save his people from their sins,"[222] as the first great mission of his life. Boldly he has invited every man to come to him, that he may remove their evil, and that they may then begin really to live,[223] and no man has accused him, on this account at least, of arrogance.

And this is his next characteristic. Really man, equal with each and all; sinless man, the implacable enemy of sin as man's one and only evil; out of these there rises up that utter truthfulness which is stamped on his whole nature, on his every word and deed. Men meet him, and read him through, and know at a glance that in him there is no

[222] Matt. 1:21.
[223] Matt. 11:28.

guile. Women, even of that pitied class that is most bitter and disillusioned, come in contact with him and at once put themselves wholly in his hands. They hear him speak, and although he does not prove or argue, although he asserts on his own authority and no more, yet they know that what he says is true. They watch him, in public and in private, working miracles and submitting to be fed, preaching to the ignorant poor and refuting learned Pharisees, and in everything, with everyone, the most convincing proof of all is his utter genuineness; in nothing is there affectation, or mere show, or double-dealing, or self-seeking, or pose, or sham, or arrogance of any kind. He hates hypocrisy — above all, when it struts and slithers in high places. From first to last, in every circumstance, he lives his life simple and true; when later he claims to be "the way, the truth, and the life,"[224] not only is no one found to contradict him, but all listen to him as if the claim he made were in harmony with what they had seen and experienced.

∞

Jesus speaks to all

Thus, by his meekness and equality with each and all, by his sinless sincerity, by his transparent truthfulness,

[224]John 14:6.

does Jesus make his way into the hearts and affections of men. The sinless find in him quick recognition and response; sinners no less quickly find in him their cure. The truthful hear in their own hearts an immediate echo to every word he says, an immediate understanding of every deed he does; the untruthful, by a kind of instinct, at once recognize in him a mortal and unyielding enemy.

But to all alike, enemies or friends, there is always the same understanding displayed, the same open frankness and simplicity. Whatever his enemies may say or do to him, before his face or covertly behind his back, his consciousness of utter truth prevents him from retaliating, from any counter-machinations, from the least attempt to overreach them, or ever to treat them otherwise than as fellowmen.

However his friends may fail or disappoint him, he endures. If one is weak and unfaithful, he will wait for him to rise: "Thou being again converted confirm thy brethren."[225] If those he trusts are not to be relied upon, still will he find cause to thank them: "You are they who have stood with me in my temptations."[226] If his enemies have their way and do him to death, still will he seek excuse for

[225] Luke 22:32.
[226] Luke 22:28.

them: "Father, forgive them, they know not what they do."[227]

No matter who they are, he understands them better than they understand themselves; the timorous he could fill with courage: "Fear not; henceforth thou shalt catch men."[228] The repentant he could fill with the joy of friendship: "Be of good heart; friend, thy sins are forgiven thee."[229] Even the unrepentant traitor he could still call "friend."[230]

Universal understanding such as this is the mother of universal sympathy. When Jesus meets a crowd, he "has compassion on them."[231] Whenever the people gather about him, in Galilee, in Decapolis, in Perea, in Judea, he must yield to them and give them all he can. And to the fascination of it they respond; among high and low, good and bad, educated and ignorant, young and old, men and women, Jew and pagan, goodwill wherever it is found no sooner comes in touch with him than it knows that it is understood, is met more than halfway, and, on its side, it knows him. We sometimes hear of men with what is

[227] Luke 23:34.
[228] Luke 5:10.
[229] Matt. 9:2.
[230] Matt. 26:50.
[231] Matt. 9:36.

called a genius for friendship; we see others who look on the power of making friends as the highest ideal of a man. In Jesus such a genius was something immediate; by those who had eyes to see, either he was at first sight known and loved, or he was known and hated.

Nowhere is this universal understanding of and sympathy with men made more manifest than in his teaching. He condescends to the lowest level of life as it is lived about him; he rises to the highest subtleties of the most sophisticated Pharisee. For his illustrations he chooses the experiences of the humblest cottager,[232] or he follows the millionaire merchant abroad[233] and goes into the houses of kings.[234] When it so suits his purpose, he uses language that the dullest yokel may understand,[235] or it will be that which shall confound the most enlightened doctor of the Law.[236] Sometimes, with noble irony, he will speak so that while the ignorant can take his words, their meaning is hidden from the wise.[237]

[232] Luke 14:8.
[233] Matt. 25:14.
[234] Luke 17:20.
[235] Luke 16:19.
[236] Matt. 19:3.
[237] Matt. 13:24.

The Good Galilean

He will rejoice with those who rejoice, with those who lament he will break down in sorrow.[238] He will praise, and he will blame;[239] he will meekly submit, and he will be stirred with indignation;[240] he will appeal, and he will threaten; he will bless, and he will curse.[241] With an ease that can come from no training, his language will express every phase of thought, will respond to every humor, and with such perfection that all literature finds no parallel. It is not only eloquence; it is utter truth that speaks, and in a manner utterly truthful, with the result that what men hear, unpretending, unaggressive, unpremeditated, spontaneous, is found to be the most perfect oratory, the most perfect use of human language that the world has ever known.

As it is with his words, so is it with his actions; in like manner does he adapt himself to all men without distinction. Universal as he is in understanding, universal in sympathy, it is inevitable that in his outpouring of himself, he should be no less universal. His miracles are worked for all alike, for strangers as well as for friends,

[238]Mark 6:31; John 11:33.
[239]Matt. 8:10; Mark 8:33.
[240]Luke 4:30; Matt. 12:31.
[241]Luke 13:34; Matt. 23:13; 25:34, 41.

good men and evil, rich as well as poor, deserving and those who had no claim. Although he declares himself to be sent "for the lost sheep of the house of Israel,"[242] and although his disciples believe that this is his only mission,[243] yet when poor pagans appeal to him, he must make exceptions — in Galilee, in the country around Tyre, and among the mountains of Decapolis.[244] He gives himself to all who seek him;[245] he dines with any who invite him: now a group of publicans in Capernaum, now a more fastidious company in Magdala, now simple women in Bethany, now cautious Pharisees in Judaea.[246]

He is as much occupied with one as with a crowd, whether that one be a ruler in Israel, or a derelict woman in Samaria, or a loathsome beggar in Jerusalem.[247] At a moment's notice, he is ready to receive a willing candidate, or, if need be, he will wait for months and even years.[248] Time seems to matter little to him, distance is not

[242] Matt. 15:24.
[243] Matt. 15:23.
[244] Matt. 8:13; 15:28, 29.
[245] Matt. 15:32.
[246] Matt. 9:10; Luke 7:36; 10:38; 11:37.
[247] John 3:1; 4:7; 5:6.
[248] Matt. 19:16; 26:50.

considered;[249] circumstances that might well make others pause with him are ignored. Men might laugh him to scorn, but he goes on doing good; they might refuse him admission to their village, but he meekly proceeds to another.[250] He will live in the midst of struggle, as well as in the house of peace;[251] he is as much at home on the steps of the Temple as with simple people in Bethany. Although he never ceases to be "Master and Lord," he is always among men as "he that serveth";[252] so much so that by a chance word we hear that he "has nowhere to lay his head."[253]

∞

Jesus shows strength and independence

On the other hand, this universal understanding, this universal sympathy and familiarity with men, never degenerates to weakness. Jesus' utter sincerity, when it speaks, makes men "astonished at his doctrine, for his speech was with power."[254] His strength in action makes them ask one

[249] Matt. 4:23.
[250] Matt. 9:24; Luke 9:53.
[251] Matt. 23:53; Luke 10:38.
[252] John 13:13.
[253] Cf. Matt. 8:20.
[254] Mark 1:27.

another, "What thing is this? What is this new doctrine? What word is this? For with authority he commandeth even the unclean spirits, and they obey him and go out."[255] Although at one time the multitudes "pressed upon him," "so that he could not go openly into the city,"[256] yet at another Jesus would so overwhelm them that they "were astonished, and were filled with fear, and wondered, and glorified God, that gave such power to men, saying, 'We have seen wonderful things today; we never saw the like."[257]

Although to his own he is lavish in kindliness and service and considerations, although he will seek any excuse to condone their shortcomings, yet when there is need, he will rebuke them with a sternness they can never forget, when they would contradict his prophecies of failure; when they were jealous; when they would lose patience with those who opposed them; when they showed ambition; when they were unforgiving; when they made little of the devotedness of children.[258]

[255] Luke 21:36.
[256] Luke 5:1; Mark 1:45.
[257] Mark 2:12; Luke 5:26.
[258] Mark 8:33; 9:38; 18:21; 19:14; 20:20; Mark 9:38; Luke 9:46.

The Good Galilean

Thus do his utter truthfulness and simplicity enable him to ride far above every inducement to weak indulgence; they make him immune from any danger of yielding to false glamour and hollow devotion. They might call him "a great prophet," and he just passes up the village out of sight in the evening twilight.[259] They might hail him "the prophet that is to come into the world," and wish to make him king, but he slips away from them all into the mountain for his evening prayer.[260] His disciples might say, "Indeed thou art the Son of God," but he knows exactly the value of their words, and when at last they have grasped their full meaning. When men cry before him, "Hosanna to the Son of David," he is not deceived; in the midst of their hosannas, he sits still, and weeps over the doom that is coming.[261]

No less does this utter truth and sincerity make him independent of those who would thwart him. He watches them gathering in numbers about him, and he does not change.[262] He reads the questionings within their hearts, which they have not the courage to speak openly, and he

[259] Luke 7:16.
[260] Matt. 14:23.
[261] Luke 19:41.
[262] Matt. 21:23.

answers them.[263] What they would conceal among themselves he brings into the light of day.[264]

They criticize his deeds or the deeds of his followers, and he corrects them. To catch him in his speech they ask him subtle questions, and he gives them their reply.[265] While he does not conceal his contempt for their meanness and their falsehood, while he warns others against the evil of their ways and example,[266] nonetheless does he deal out to them unlimited patience and forbearance. Let one of them speak the truth from his heart, and at once he is approved and encouraged.[267]

In all the pictures of the character of Jesus, there is no feature more astonishing than this constant, unflinching endurance of his enemies, his constant entrusting of himself into their hands, even after he has been compelled to confute them, publicly to denounce them, to put them to shame before their own disciples, to defy them in their own court,[268] to call them to their faces "hypocrites," to warn

[263] Matt. 9:4.
[264] Luke 12:2.
[265] Matt. 9:14; Mark 12:13.
[266] Matt. 15:7; Mark 4:24.
[267] Mark 12:32.
[268] Luke 11:17; Matt. 15:12; Mark 12:15; John 7:28.

the people against their example, and his own against their falsehood and deceit.[269] In spite of all this, he would continue to go to them; to none does he make more fervent appeal; the last days of his life are devoted wholly to them. And they in their turn would continue to come to him; the fascination drew them, they would invite him to sit with them at table; at times one or another among them would break out and acknowledge that indeed he was the speaker of truth.[270]

Jesus is a model of prayer and virtue

But to those who lived close beside him, it was not difficult to discover the secret of this independence. He was with men and among them, but in a true sense he was not of them; while he lived their life to the full, and "bore their sorrows and carried their griefs"[271] more than they carried them themselves, nevertheless, within him and all about him, for those who were familiar with him to see, there was another life and another atmosphere far more real and far more intense than anything this earth had to

[269]Matt. 16:6; 22:18; 23:2.
[270]Luke 11:37; Mark 12:32.
[271]Cf. Isa. 53:4.

give him. It was his life of prayer, and with it, as a consequence, his constant preference for solitude.

His friends soon learned to respect his hours of prayer in the morning and evening; when they awoke at dawn and he was not among them, they knew where they would find him.[272] After sunset he had regular places for his prayer. When he went apart to spend a night in prayer, they would understand and let him go; if he would take them, they would readily go with him.[273]

Often whole days would pass by, and days would grow into weeks, and he would do apparently nothing. Crowds would gather around him, and he would retire from them to pray, up the mountainside or into desert places.[274] They would become enthusiastic and wish to make him king, and he would fly "into the mountain alone, to pray." Or they would desert him, and he would not seem to mind; in the morning his friends would find him lost in prayer.[275] During all his long tour, extending to months, outside the borders of Palestine there is no record of a single sermon preached or public demonstration made; his time would

---

[272] Mark 1:35-36.
[273] Luke 6:12; 9:28; 22:39.
[274] Luke 5:16; 6:12.
[275] Luke 11:1.

seem to have been spent in continual prayer. He is at prayer among the hills of Decapolis when the people find him out.[276] It is after prayer, a few days later, that he asks Simon the momentous question: "Who do you say that I am?"

Such was the fact, which those who lived with him soon understood, and accepted, and in their feeble way aspired to imitate, and which this man of utter simplicity and truth never made an effort to conceal. The atmosphere of prayer, the retirement apart from men, the personal dealing with the Father at all times: these were the features that most struck those who were most with Jesus. God the Father, the beginning and the end, and therefore all that came between; the will of the Father, and that alone, giving everything else its significance, every success, every failure, everything we do and are: this was Jesus' only perspective, and its constant repetition, not so much as a doctrine to be taught, but as a truth to be assumed, runs through his life from first to last:

- "I must be about my Father's business."[277]

- "My meat is to do the will of him that sent me."[278]

[276] Matt. 15:29.
[277] Luke 2:49.
[278] Luke 4:34.

Jesus Is an Example of Every Perfection

- "As the Father hath given me commandment, so do I."[279]

- "Heavenly Father, I give thee thanks."[280]

- "Father, save me from this hour."[281]

- "Father, not my will but thine be done."[282]

- "I have glorified thee on the earth, I have finished the work thou gavest me to do."[283]

- "Father, into thy hands I commend my spirit."[284]

- "As the Father hath sent me, I also send you."[285]

The life of the soul expressed in these and many more successive cries is unmistakable.

We must come to an end. Hitherto we have marked certain outlines that may help to distinguish the character of Jesus as it revealed itself among men; when we endeavor to descend more to details, when we ask ourselves

[279] John 14:31.
[280] John 11:41.
[281] John 12:27.
[282] Luke 22:42.
[283] John 17:4.
[284] Luke 23:46.
[285] John 20:21.

what were his particular virtues, we are unable to proceed. He had no one virtue in particular, because he had them all; and he had them in so perfect a balance, so much part of his very human nature, that they passed by unnoticed among men. And this we say, not because, knowing who he was — the Son of God made man — we believe that it must have been so, but because it is written in the actual portrait of the man as the Evangelists have drawn it out for us.

We mark the virtues of other men, and we see them to be reflections of the same in him; we go to the theologians, and we find that what they teach of the virtues finds its best illustrations in his life. Whenever he himself speaks of virtue, we know, and the men who listened to him knew, that the model of it all was to be found in him. Thus, he enumerates the Beatitudes, and as he does so, he draws a picture of himself. In the rest of the Sermon on the Mount, he speaks of forgiveness and innocence, of simplicity in speech, of generosity, of forbearance, of hidden well-doing, of prayer, of trust in God, of contempt of earthly things, of mercy in judgment, of fidelity; and all who hear him see him to be a model of all that he demands. He declares himself to be the exemplar for all men, not in this virtue or that, but in that which is fundamental to all virtues: "Learn of me, because I am meek and humble of heart,"[286] and not a voice is raised in protest; the whole tenor of his life is proof enough that what he says is true.

∞

Jesus is the best example of love

But at the last — for to us it is evident even more than it might perhaps have been to those who thronged close about him — the virtue that in Jesus was the source of and the key to all the rest was his unbounded love. Love was at the root of his universal understanding and his universal sympathy. Love made him pour himself out on all the world. What attracted men to him, what made "all the world go after him,"[287] although they did not know it, was the fascination of his love. Love as he taught it was a new thing in the world. Love as he practiced it has made the world another place. With him and his interpretation of it, it became indeed "a new commandment," however ancient might be the words in which it was set.

When later the Apostles looked back, and pieced the whole picture together, it was this tremendous love of Jesus which grew upon them, swallowing up all the rest:

[286]Matt. 11:29.
[287]Cf. John 12:19.

The Good Galilean

"Having loved his own that were in the world, he loved them unto the end."[288] The memory of this was their abiding consolation and encouragement for all time, both to him who could call himself "the disciple whom Jesus loved," and to him who could remember that he had one day made a last profession of love for his Master and it had been accepted.[289]

To illustrate this, even inadequately, it would be necessary to pass again through the whole life of Jesus upon earth; for love reveals itself on every page, consistently the same, however different in its manifestation.

But on this very account there is no need to say more; if ever in the word *love* has been associated with the name of any man upon this earth, it is with the name of Jesus Christ. When St. Paul endeavored to express Jesus to himself, he could only sum him up by speaking of his love.[290] When, since his time, Fathers and Doctors and theologians and saints have tried to do likewise, they have one and all ended on the same theme.

Or conversely, when St. Paul speaks of love in detail and would endeavor to describe to the people of Corinth

[288]John 13:1.
[289]John 21:15-17, 20.
[290]Rom. 8:35-39.

this new power that has come into the world, he can only keep the Model before his eyes; when he has ended, what has he done but portray one aspect of him?

> Jesus is patient,
> Is kind.
> Jesus envieth not,
> Dealeth not perversely,
> Is not puffed up,
> Is not ambitious,
> Seeketh not his own,
> Is not provoked to anger,
> Thinketh no evil,
> Rejoiceth not in iniquity,
> But rejoiceth with the truth,
> Beareth all things,
> Believeth all things,
> Hopeth all things,
> Endureth all things.[291]

True, the description is inadequate; the picture given is rather negative than positive; but as with God we can more easily say what he is not than what he is, so is it in our effort to describe even the human love of Jesus Christ.

[291] Cf. 1 Cor. 13:4-7.

The Good Galilean

St. Peter, it would seem, can do no better, for he says:

> Christ also suffered for us,
> Leaving you an example
> That you should follow his steps;
> Who did no sin,
> Neither was guile found in his mouth;
> Who when he was reviled,
> Did not revile;
> When he suffered,
> He threatened not,
> But delivered himself
> To him that judged him unjustly.[292]

If St. Paul and St. Peter can scarcely speak of Jesus and his love in anything but negatives; if the former by the simple thought, "The Son of God loved me and gave himself for me"[293] is struck dumb, how can anyone else in this world hope to describe Jesus or his love? It is enough to use the words of Jesus himself: "Greater love than this no man hath, that he lay down his life for his friend,"[294] and to realize how completely he has fulfilled this in himself, not

[292] 1 Pet. 2:21-23.
[293] Gal. 2:20.
[294] John 15:13.

on Calvary alone, but in every moment of his days on earth, and even to this day in heaven: "Always living to make intercession for us,"[295] "with us all days, even to the consummation of the world."[296]

295 Heb. 7:25.
296 Matt. 28:20.

Biographical note

∞

Alban Goodier

Alban Goodier was a Jesuit who served for a time as archbishop of Bombay, India. He was renowned for his memorable aphorisms: "A friend is the one who comes in when the whole world has gone out"; "The enthusiastic, to those who are not, are always something of a trial"; and many more.

He was a well-respected writer who contributed many articles to the magazine *The Messenger of the Sacred Heart*. He wrote more than a dozen books, including *The Meaning of Life*, *Saints for Sinners*, *The Passion and Death of Our Lord Jesus Christ*, and *The Inner Life of the Catholic*.

An Invitation

Reader, the book that you hold in your hands was published by Sophia Institute Press.

Sophia Institute seeks to restore man's knowledge of eternal truth, including man's knowledge of his own nature, his relation to other persons, and his relation to God.

Our press fulfills this mission by offering translations, reprints, and new publications. We offer scholarly as well as popular publications; there are works of fiction along with books that draw from all the arts and sciences of our civilization. These books afford readers a rich source of the enduring wisdom of mankind.

Sophia Institute Press is the publishing arm of the Thomas More College of Liberal Arts and Holy Spirit College. Both colleges are dedicated to providing university-level education in the Western tradition under the guiding light of Catholic teaching.

If you know a young person who might be interested in the ideas found in this book, share it. If you know a young person seeking a college that takes seriously the adventure of learning and the quest for truth, bring our institutions to his attention.

www.SophiaInstitute.com
www.ThomasMoreCollege.edu
www.HolySpiritCollege.org

SOPHIA INSTITUTE PRESS

THE PUBLISHING DIVISION OF